To my grandchildren: Kate, Elizabeth, Grace, Philip, Richard, and Sam —L. C.

For Our Children —G. H.

Acknowledgments

The talented Greg Harlin has created magnificent illustrations for this book, and I am grateful to him, as I know generations of children and parents will be. I also want to give special thanks to my research assistant at the American Enterprise Institute, Cristina Allegretti, for the keen intelligence she brought to every search for facts and sources, as well as for her wonderfully patient attention to detail. I'd like to acknowledge as well the fine work of Pamela Ronsaville, Greg Harlin's agent, who did so much work to coordinate his efforts and mine.

Three of my AEI colleagues, Walter Berns, Robert Goldwin, and James Wilson, were kind enough to read a draft manuscript of this book, and I thank them for their wise suggestions. Kathryn Duryea, Danny Laurence, Amanda Fritsch, and Luci Hague also provided valuable assistance on this project. In addition, I want to thank Chris DeMuth, AEI president, for his guidance. He has been a thoughtful and thoroughly inspiring leader.

My gratitude to the entire publishing team at Simon & Schuster, beginning at the top with Carolyn Reidy, Rick Richter, and Rubin Pfeffer. Paula Wiseman, combining thoughtfulness and insight, is a spectacular editor, and her contributions to this book are too many to count. I would also like to thank Dorothy Gribbin and Alexandra Penfold for their editorial contributions, and Lizzy Bromley for her artful eye. She, Dan Potash, and Chloë Foglia have helped create a beautiful book. Lisa Ford, Chava Wolin, Paul Crichton, Mary McAveney, Michelle Montague, Michelle Fadlalla, and Karen Frangipane have all been important to *We the People*, and I admire their dedication—and the dedication of all in Simon & Schuster's Children's Division—to bringing good books to the next generation of leaders for this country and the world.

Attorney Bob Barnett has for the seventh time in the past seven years helped me bring a book project from beginning to completion, and I would like once again to thank him for being a deeply skilled, thoroughly knowledgeable, and always genial guide. —L. C.

SIMON & SCHUSTER BOOKS FOR YOUNG READERS
An imprint of Simon & Schuster Children's Publishing Division
1230 Avenue of the Americas, New York, New York 10020
Text copyright © 2008 by Lynne V. Cheney
Illustrations copyright © 2008 by Greg Harlin
All rights reserved, including the right of reproduction in whole or in part in any form.
SIMON & SCHUSTER BOOKS FOR YOUNG READERS is a trademark of Simon & Schuster, Inc.
The text for this book is set in Celestia Antique.
The illustrations for this book were created with various water media on watercolor paper.
Manufactured in China

20 19 18 17 16 15 14 13 12 11   0621 SCP
Library of Congress Cataloging-in-Publication Data
Cheney, Lynne V.
We the people : the story of our Constitution / by Lynne Cheney ; illustrated by Greg Harlin.
p. cm.
ISBN-13: 978-1-4169-5418-7 (hardcover) • ISBN-13: 978-1-4424-4422-5 (paperback)
1. United States. Constitution—Juvenile literature. 2. United States—Politics and government—1775-1783—Juvenile literature. 3. United States—Politics and government—1783-1789—Juvenile literature. 4. Constitutional history—United States—Juvenile literature. I. Harlin, Greg, ill. II. Title.
E303.C48 2008 • 342.7302'9—dc22
2008008871

Editor's Note: Archaic spelling, capitalization, and punctuation in historical quotations have been modernized throughout the text.

We the People

The Story of Our Constitution

BY

LYNNE CHENEY

ILLUSTRATED BY

GREG HARLIN

SIMON & SCHUSTER BOOKS FOR YOUNG READERS
New York   London   Toronto   Sydney

"The happy union of these states is a wonder; their Constitution a miracle; their example the hope of liberty throughout the world."

—James Madison

When 1787 began, our young country was in turmoil. The central government was unable to pay off debts, there was armed insurrection in Massachusetts, and foreign governments were taking advantage of our weakness. The question of the hour, James Madison wrote, was "whether the American experiment was to be a blessing to the world or to blast forever the hopes which the republican cause had inspired."

The framers of the Constitution made it a blessing, creating a new and stronger American union and flying in the face of prevailing wisdom as they did so. In the eighteenth century, representative government in a nation of vast scale was thought impossible, a recipe for chaos and confusion; but an extended republic based on popular sovereignty was exactly what the Constitution created in Philadelphia in the summer of 1787 envisaged. The government based upon it has now endured more than 220 years.

The story of our founding document is an important one for our children to know. It is a tale of persistence, as delegates kept on despite obstacles that at times made their task seem impossible. It is a tale of creativity, with the delegates providing a framework for a government entirely new. It is also a story that makes clear there was nothing inevitable about the Constitution that emerged from the Philadelphia convention. History might have gone otherwise but for the framers' genius, and we should be grateful for James Madison, George Washington, Benjamin Franklin, and the others who gathered in Philadelphia. We should be grateful as well for men and women such as Frederick Douglass, Elizabeth Cady Stanton, and Martin Luther King Jr., who in later centuries took up the work of the founders, making the union formed in 1787 the more perfect one we know today.

Lynne Cheney

Astride his favorite horse, Nelson, General George Washington looked on as thousands of British soldiers marched out of Yorktown, Virginia, to lay down their arms. It was October 19, 1781, and America, with help from France, had just won the battle that would end the Revolutionary War.

For the British the loss was a shock. Theirs was the mightiest army in the world, and they had thought it impossible that the Americans would defeat them. According to tradition the soldiers marching out of Yorktown to surrender played a song called "The World Turned Upside Down."

For citizens of our country, living on a vast and bountiful continent, it seemed a new age was dawning. A free and independent America would surely prosper and become a great and mighty nation.

"The citizens of America . . . are from this period to be considered as the actors on a most conspicuous theater, which seems to be peculiarly designated by Providence for the display of human greatness and felicity."
GEORGE WASHINGTON

But over the next several years, trouble became apparent. America had adopted rules for governing called the Articles of Confederation, and they didn't work very well. Congress, which was supposed to be in charge of the confederation, or union, of states, did not have enough power. It could not prevent states from printing their own money. It could not get them to help defend America or to pay off debts from the Revolutionary War. Other countries, sensing the weakness of the United States, took advantage. The British refused to move out of military posts they were supposed to give up after the Revolutionary War.

In Massachusetts farmers who couldn't pay their debts rose up against the government. When they tried to seize a building in Springfield where guns and ammunition were kept, militia fired upon them. Americans were killing Americans. Was our country, which had so recently won its independence, now going to come apart?

—

"I am mortified beyond expression when I view the clouds which have spread over the brightest morn that ever dawned upon any country."
GEORGE WASHINGTON

—

In 1787 delegates from twelve states traveled to a convention in Philadelphia to figure out a better plan for governing the country. Congress had instructed them to revise the Articles of Confederation, but some were thinking well beyond that. James Madison of Virginia, the first delegate to arrive from out of town, had studied how nations worked and was convinced America needed a much stronger government than the Articles could provide—and soon. The current government, he believed, was near collapse.

In his room at a Philadelphia boardinghouse, Madison, a small man of great learning, labored over a plan to present to the convention. His boldest idea was that the nation's government start with the people. As it was, state legislatures were choosing the members of Congress. Madison proposed that the people have a direct say in who represented them.

"The great fabric to be raised would be more stable and durable if it should rest on the solid foundation of the people themselves."
JAMES MADISON

George Washington, who had returned to
private life after the Revolutionary War,
arrived in Philadelphia on May 13, the
day before the convention was scheduled
to begin. Although he didn't like leaving
his beloved home at Mount Vernon,
Washington came to the convention
because he was worried. Thirteen states,
all pulling in different directions, were
bringing ruin upon America, he believed.

Bells rang out to celebrate Washington's
arrival, and joyful crowds gathered to greet
him. The people of Philadelphia remembered
how this tall, dignified man had persisted in
the darkest hours of the Revolution, when
it had seemed impossible that America
would win her war for independence.
They remembered how he had given up
power after the war when some had wanted
to make him a king. All across America
he was loved and respected, which made
his presence in Philadelphia especially
important. With him at the convention,
Americans were more likely to look
favorably upon what the delegates decided.

—

"To the man who unites all hearts."
A POPULAR TOAST OF THE TIME,
OFFERED TO HONOR
GEORGE WASHINGTON

—

Not until May 25—eleven days after the convention was supposed to start—were there enough delegates for it to begin. Twenty-nine men gathered in the Pennsylvania State House, elected George Washington the convention's president, and made rules, including one that pledged them all to secrecy.

James Madison had used the time leading up to the convention to present his ideas to his fellow Virginians, and on May 29 one of the Virginia representatives proposed Madison's plan to the assembled delegates. As Madison, seated close to George Washington, took notes, Governor Edmund Randolph described a government of three branches: legislative, or the Congress; judicial, or the courts; and a national executive. The legislative branch would have two parts, or houses, with the people of each state electing the members of the first house. Some delegates argued that the people couldn't be trusted to choose their representatives, but most disagreed. They thought that the place for government to begin was with the people.

"*The national legislative powers ought to flow immediately from the people.*"
James Wilson
Delegate from Pennsylvania

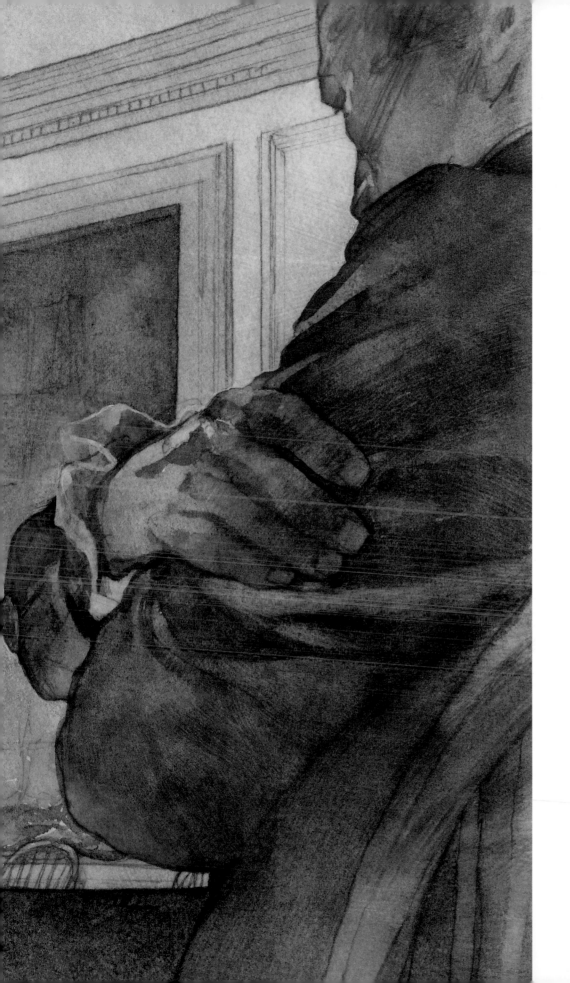

What nearly brought the convention to an end was the idea of the large states becoming more powerful. Under the Articles of Confederation, every state had one vote, but the Virginia Plan gave more representatives and more votes to states with more people. Delegates from large states—Virginia, Pennsylvania, and Massachusetts—thought that was only fair, but delegates from small states believed that their interests would be trampled upon.

William Paterson of New Jersey, scolding the delegates for going so far beyond the Articles of Confederation, presented a plan that preserved equality in voting. It was rejected, but the small states would not give up and delegates continued to argue bitterly.

"We would sooner submit to a foreign power than submit to be deprived of an equality of suffrage."
JOHN DICKINSON
DELEGATE FROM DELAWARE

The oldest delegate was inventor and statesman Benjamin Franklin. At eighty-one, he had trouble walking and was carried in a sedan chair from his home to the convention.

Franklin commanded great respect, but not even he could get quarreling delegates to put their anger aside. Through most of June they fought, their tempers made worse by hot weather. It was sweltering as Roger Sherman of Connecticut proposed that in one house of the legislature, states be represented according to size and in the other, the Senate, each state have an equal number of votes. But the idea went nowhere. Large states were not willing to give up anything to smaller ones.

Dr. Franklin suggested that the delegates send for a chaplain to lead them in prayer. The leaders of the Revolution had sought God's help, he said, and so should those who were trying to build a new nation.

"How has it happened . . . that we have not hitherto once thought of humbly applying to the Father of lights to illuminate our understandings?"
BENJAMIN FRANKLIN
DELEGATE FROM PENNSYLVANIA

The delegates did not send for a chaplain, but as the Fourth of July neared, they did stop arguing long enough to appoint a committee to seek a way out of their difficulties. Acting on a suggestion by Dr. Franklin, the committee crafted what became known as the Great Compromise. It made Mr. Sherman's proposal more appealing to large states by having all legislation concerning money begin in the first house of the legislature, where big states had more power.

One evening in his garden, Dr. Franklin showed visitors a curiosity someone had sent him, a two-headed snake preserved in a vial. Such a creature made the point, he said, that compromise was often crucial to progress.

—

"The doctor mentioned the situation of this snake, if . . . one head should choose to go on one side of the stem of a bush and the other head should prefer the other side, and . . . neither of the heads would consent to come back or give way to the other."
MANASSEH CUTLER
ONE OF FRANKLIN'S VISITORS

—

But when the committee took its suggestion for compromise back to the convention, delegates from large states still resisted. Gouverneur Morris of Pennsylvania, a tall commanding man with a wooden leg, was particularly angry that small states were threatening to form a separate union unless there was equal voting in the Senate. The country would be united one way or another, he said, offering a threat of his own: "If persuasion does not unite it, the sword will."

Delegates also fell to quarreling about who should be counted in order to figure out how many representatives a state should have. Southerners wanted to count slaves so that their states would have more representatives. Northerners, especially those who hated slavery, objected, not wanting to give the South more power.

It seemed as though the convention might fall apart, and with it, the country.

"*I almost despair.*"
GEORGE WASHINGTON

With failure looming, a few delegates had a change of heart. In a close and momentous vote on July 16, the convention adopted the Great Compromise. In one house states would be represented according to population, and in the other they would have an equal number of votes.

To determine how many representatives a state would have, the convention decided to count three fifths of the slaves. This compromise meant that the South would be part of the new government, but some delegates hated the bargain. Slavery was an evil institution, Gouverneur Morris raged, "the curse of heaven on the states where it prevailed."

Such words would ring out in the State House again when the delegates debated a ban on bringing more slaves into the country. The convention decided that there could be no ban for twenty years.

———

"[Slaves] bring the judgment of heaven on a country."
GEORGE MASON
DELEGATE FROM VIRGINIA

———

The delegates moved on to other decisions, and by July 26 they were ready to have a group called the Committee of Detail go to work. Organizing the points that the delegates had agreed to, the members of the committee, headed by John Rutledge of South Carolina, wrote the first draft of the Constitution. They named parts of government and certain offices that the delegates had created, calling the first house of Congress the House of Representatives and its leader the speaker. They called the highest body in the judicial branch the Supreme Court and named the head of the executive branch the president of the United States.

While members of the committee were at work, other delegates took a break. George Washington went fishing.

"*Went up to one Jane Moore's in the vicinity of Valley Forge to get trout.*"
GEORGE WASHINGTON

We the People of the United States, in Order to form a more perfect Union, establish Justice, insure domestic Tranquility, provide for the common defence, promote the general Welfare, and secure the Blessings of Liberty to ourselves and our Posterity, do ordain and establish this Constitution for the United States of America

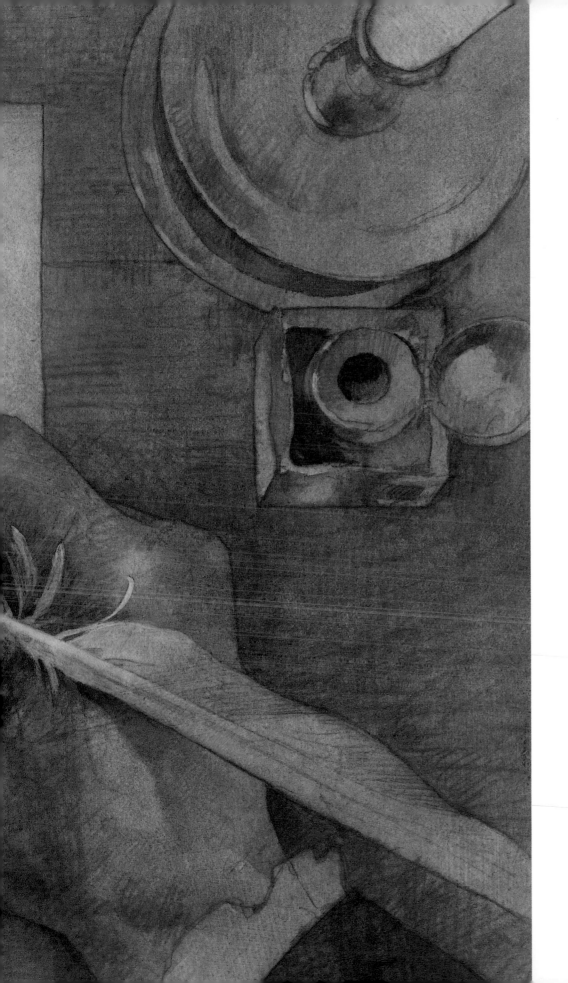

Gathering again on August 6 to talk about the draft Constitution, delegates soon took up a question they had discussed many times before: How should the president be elected? Should state legislatures make the choice? Or members of Congress? They finally agreed on a system of electors that would allow the president to be chosen, indirectly, by the people.

The delegates also decided that the people should be in charge of ratifying the Constitution. Rather than seek the approval of state legislatures, delegates chose to submit the Constitution to specially elected conventions in every state. When the Committee of Style and Arrangement—the delegates assigned to write the final version of the Constitution—got to work, they emphasized at the beginning of the document that the Constitution would become supreme law only when the people decided it should be so.

"This Constitution . . . is laid before the citizens of the United States. . . . By their fiat, it will become of value and authority."
JAMES WILSON

On September 17, after the final draft of the Constitution was read aloud, Benjamin Franklin addressed the convention. He told the delegates that there were parts of the document with which he did not agree but that over a long life he had learned he was not always right. On the whole, he said, the Constitution was astonishingly good, and he hoped that other delegates who had doubts would join him in signing it. Several refused, including Elbridge Gerry of Massachusetts and George Mason of Virginia, who wanted the Constitution explicitly to set forth the rights of individuals.

George Washington, as president of the convention, was the first to put his name to the Constitution, then thirty-seven others followed, state by state. As the last delegate signed the document, Dr. Franklin looked at the sun painted on the back of George Washington's chair and saw in it a sign of a new beginning for America.

—

"At length I have the happiness to know that it is a rising and not a setting sun."
BENJAMIN FRANKLIN

—

By July 4, 1788, the people of ten states had, after sometimes fierce debate, ratified the Constitution. Since only nine states were required to make the Constitution the supreme law of the country, it was time for a celebration. In Philadelphia, after early morning bells and a cannon salute, crowds lined the streets to watch high-stepping horses lead a parade of flags, bands, and floats. The Grand Federal Edifice, a specially constructed building honoring the union, passed by, pulled by ten white horses. A carved and painted twenty-gun ship, the *Union*, made its way through town on its carriage.

Citizens of every occupation marched, weavers followed by chair makers, bricklayers, and gilders; bookbinders by coppersmiths and clergymen. And at the end of the parade came feasting and an oration. "Happy country!" proclaimed convention delegate James Wilson. "May thy happiness be perpetual!"

—

"'Tis done! We have become a nation."
BENJAMIN RUSH
CITIZEN OF PENNSYLVANIA—
AND OF THE UNITED STATES OF AMERICA

—

$\mathcal{U}$nder the Constitution, America would become the nation George Washington imagined, a place of freedom in which people can aspire to high goals and seek happiness, a country exemplifying the blessings of ordered liberty.

But the Constitution that the delegates signed in Philadelphia in 1787 was not perfect, and being aware of that, delegates included in the Constitution ways of changing or amending it. The first ten amendments, called the Bill of Rights, were passed by two thirds of the Congress in 1789 and ratified by three fourths of the states in 1791. Providing protection for the many rights we have as individuals, they include safeguards for freedoms of speech, religion, and the press. Amendments added after the Civil War did away with slavery and provided that the right to vote will not be restricted on account of race. In 1920 the Constitution was amended to recognize the right of women to vote.

The document created in Philadelphia in 1787 has changed as our country has changed, growing in justice over the years. Once there were Americans who looked at the Constitution and did not see themselves. Today "We the people" includes all of us, working together, to make our great country greater still.

SOURCES

The U.S. Constitution is on public display at the National Archives and Records Administration in Washington, D.C. A transcription of the original Constitution indicating where that document has been amended or superseded can be found at www.archives.gov/exhibits/charters/constitution_transcript .html. The National Constitution Center provides interactive tools for exploring the Constitution at www.constitutioncenter.org.

epigraph Madison's words, from September 1829, can be found in the Web edition of *The Founders' Constitution*, edited by Philip B. Kurland and Ralph Lerner, at http ://press-pubs.uchicago.edu/founders/documents/v1ch7s27.html.

5 George Washington's words, from a 1783 letter he sent to the thirteen states, can be found in the George Washington Papers, made available in searchable form by the Library of Congress at www.memory.loc.gov/ammem/gwhtml/gwhome.html.

6 George Washington's words, from an October 31, 1786, letter to Henry Lee, can be found in the George Washington Papers.

9 Only twelve states were represented at the convention because Rhode Island refused to send delegates.

James Madison's words are from the extensive notes he took at the convention. His notes, as well as those of other delegates mentioned below, can be found in Max Farrand's *The Records of the Federal Convention of 1787*, a four-volume work published in 1911. The Library of Congress has made three of the four volumes available in searchable form at www.memory.loc.gov/ammem/amlaw/lwfr.html.

10 Among those accompanying Washington was William Lee, an enslaved man who acted as Washington's valet. About a third of the delegates to the convention were slave owners, including every delegate from Virginia.

In 1789, when Washington toured New England, Boston citizens put the words of the toast "To the man who unites all hearts" atop a triumphal arch. Washington recorded their efforts in his diary for October 24. This entry can be found in the George Washington Papers.

12 Over the course of the nearly four month-long convention, a total of fifty-five delegates would attend. The Pennsylvania State House is called Independence Hall today.

Madison's leadership in crafting the Virginia Plan that Randolph introduced is one of the reasons he is often referred to as the Father of the Constitution. The careful notes he took provide us with our fullest record of the convention. They were published in 1840.

James Wilson's words are from notes taken by Robert Yates of New York.

15 John Dickinson's words are from notes taken by Madison.

16 Benjamin Franklin's words are from notes taken by Madison.

18 The words of Manasseh Cutler, who visited Franklin at the time of the convention, are from a journal he kept. His description of his visit can be found in Farrand's *Records of the Federal Convention*.

21 Gouverneur Morris's words are from notes taken by Madison.

George Washington's words are from a letter to Alexander Hamilton that can be found in the George Washington Papers.

22 Gouverneur Morris's words are from notes taken by Madison.

George Mason's words are from notes taken by Madison.

24 George Washington actually went fishing twice during this break, the first time for trout in Pennsylvania. Being near Valley Forge, he visited the place where he and his men had spent the hard winter of 1777. The second time he went fishing, he was outside Trenton, New Jersey.

George Washington's words, from his diary, can be found in the George Washington Papers.

27 The indirect election of the president was accomplished by having each state choose a number of electors equaling its number of representatives and senators. The electors, in turn, vote for president. The Constitution left it up to the states to decide on the method for choosing electors. By 1836 every state except South Carolina had electors chosen by statewide popular vote.

James Wilson's words, part of the case he made for the Constitution in the Pennsylvania ratifying convention, can be found in Jonathan Elliot's five-volume work, *The Debates in the Several State Conventions on the Adoption of the Federal Constitution*, published between 1836 and 1845 and made available by the Library of Congress in searchable form at www.memory.loc.gov/ammem/amlaw/lwed.html.

Gouverneur Morris, chosen to write the final draft of the Constitution, penned the fine expression of national purpose in the preamble, which is illustrated.

28 George Read of Delaware signed for his colleague John Dickinson, who was ill. Thus, there are thirty-nine delegate signatures on the Constitution.

Benjamin Franklin's words are from notes taken by Madison.

30 James Madison played a crucial role in the ratification of the Constitution, joining together with Alexander Hamilton and John Jay, both of New York, to write the Federalist Papers, a series of essays that appeared in New York newspapers and made the case for ratification. The Federalist Papers are available in searchable form at the Avalon Project at Yale Law School, www.yale.edu /lawweb/avalon/federal/fed.htm. Madison was also the principal author of the Bill of Rights, the first ten amendments to the Constitution.

Francis Hopkinson organized and made a record of the festivities, including James Wilson's speech. His account can be found in *The Miscellaneous Essays and Occasional Writings of Francis Hopkinson, Esq.*, vol. 2 (Philadelphia: Printed by T. Dobson, 1792), 349–422. *Miscellaneous Essays* is available as a Google book at http://books.google .com.

Benjamin Rush's words, from a July 9, 1788, letter to Elias Boudinot, appear in Lyman H. Butterfield's *Letters of Benjamin Rush*, vol. 1 (Princeton, NJ: Princeton University Press, 1951), 475.